MW00769092

© 2002 by Barbour Publishing, Inc.

ISBN 1-58660-088-5

All Scripture quotations are taken from the King James Version of the Bible.

Selections by Mary Herron and Donna Lange are used with the authors' permission.

Published by Barbour Publishing, Inc., P.O. Box 719, Uhrichsville, Ohio 44683
http://www.barbourbooks.com

 Member of the
Evangelical Christian
Publishers Association

Printed in China.

Sweets
FOR MY SWEET

A CELEBRATION OF LOVE
AND CHOCOLATE

ELLYN SANNA

BARBOUR
PUBLISHING, INC.

One of the greatest treasures ever discovered was the bean from the tree Theobroma cacao, *the original source of chocolate. Smooth in texture, intense in taste, subtly perfumed, and elegant to behold, chocolate is a rich source of sensory pleasure, adored by almost everyone.*

CHRISTINE MCFADDEN AND CHRISTINE FRANCE

*The knowledge that you love me,
that I love you. . .how sweet!
Each day I feel that knowledge
seeping through my heart,
the way a piece of chocolate dissolves in my mouth,
filling me with a dark, mysterious, sweetness.*

GWYNETH GAVIN

CONTENTS

'Tis you alone that sweetens life. . . .

JOHN HERVEY

*Better is a dinner of herbs where love is,
than a stalled ox and hatred therewith.*

PROVERBS 15:17

1

The Sweet Language of Love

We are all pencils in the hands of a writing God,
who is sending love letters to the world.

MOTHER TERESA

Love is a short word, but it contains all:
it means the body, the soul, the life, the entire being. . . .

GUY DE MAUPASSANT

Chocolate is a universal symbol of love. Ever since its discovery by the Aztecs in ancient Mexico, it has been used as a gift—a concrete expression of a thousand feelings too sweet, too complex for mere words.

Love needs a tangible language, for love cannot be contained nor expressed by even the most sophisticated vocabulary. Music expresses love to our ears. . .flowers are a visual symbol of our feelings. . .and chocolate allows us to taste love's sweetness.

Love is my life,
Life is my love,
Love is my whole felicity,
Love is my sweet,
Sweet is my love,
I am in love,
And love in me.

MICHAEL DRAYTON

Nothing is sweeter than love, nothing higher,
nothing broader, nothing better, either in heaven or earth:
because love is born of God.

THOMAS Á KEMPIS

My Valentine

In 1956, boys were not allowed in the girls' dorm—not even on Valentine's Day. When the doorbell rang, the closest girl answered, then yelled a name up the stairs.

I'd been listening for my name all day. One by one, all the other girls had been summoned through the big Victorian doorway to receive their valentines. Now curfew was almost upon us—and I still hadn't heard my name.

For almost a year, Danny and I had double-dated with some friends. He would often stop by the snack bar where I worked, and we would chat about our times together. One day recently, he had asked me if I were going to an out-of-town basketball game. I hated to admit I hadn't been invited, but when I did, he burst out, "Why don't you go with me?"

That was our first "real" date, just him and me alone. It didn't take many more before I was sure there was something special between us. I had dreamed for days of the beautiful valentine he would give me; I had imagined the sweet words it might say.

But instead, I had received nothing at all. I had almost given up hope when I heard my name echo down the hallway.

I tried to look calm as I descended the spiral staircase that lead down to the entryway. As I neared the bottom, I saw Danny looking up at me—but all I could see was the satin, heart-shaped box he was holding. It was so large that the ribbons spilled down over his arm.

Danny started to explain why he was so late, but before he could say more than a few words, the dorm mother's door opened. "Good night, Danny," she said firmly as the curfew bell rang.

He thrust the box into my hands, then quickly drew me close. "You will always be my valentine," he whispered.

As the door closed behind him, the dorm mother smiled at me. "That's a pretty impressive box. Looks serious, I would say."

I drifted up the stairs, replaying his words in my ear. *You will always be my valentine.*

When I reached my room, I wanted to hug my dreams close to me in silence—but my roommates saw the enormous box of chocolate, and they immediately had other ideas. Gently, reverently, I began to open the beautiful heart, but the other girls caught the aroma of chocolate, and their eager hands tugged the cover free. We had never seen so much chocolate. I snapped out of my hazy dream and joined the fun as we feasted on those delicious, dark morsels.

Many years have come and gone since that day, but the memory has never faded. Each year as Valentine's Day approaches, I remember that heart-shaped, five-pound box of chocolate with its trailing satin ribbons. And just as sweet as that long-ago chocolate is the knowledge I have today—*I am still Danny's Valentine.*

MARY HERRON

Give thy heart's best treasure,
And the more thou spendest
From thy little store,
With a double bounty,
God will give thee more.

ADELAIDE A. PROCTOR

The honey of the Hybla bees
Is not so sweet as kissing you. . . .

SAMUEL HOFFENSTEIN

Sensations sweet,
Felt in the blood and felt along the heart.

WILLIAM WORDSWORTH

One may give without loving;
but none can love without giving.

ANONYMOUS

Love is, above all, the gift of oneself.

JEAN ANOUILH

Happy Valentine's Day

"Bye, honey." Jack's kiss was so quick Meg barely felt the brush of his lips against hers. Before she could say anything, he was gone, the door shut tight behind him. She heard the sound of his car pulling out of the driveway, then she was all alone, except for their three children still sleeping in their beds.

"Happy Valentine's Day," she said to the empty house. She sighed and went down to the basement to do a load of laundry.

All too soon, the children would be awake. With three kids under five, two still in diapers, Meg wouldn't have time to miss Jack while he was gone on a business trip. She wouldn't pine for him the way she used to before the kids were born, longing for his arms, her heart leaping when the phone rang. He would call tonight, she knew, and he would tell her he loved her–but really, what difference did it make? Jack's love wouldn't make her any less exhausted after spending the day chasing toddlers; his love wouldn't make her feel beautiful and exciting the way it once had.

No, those days were gone. These days, Meg didn't feel like anyone's lover; instead, she was a worn-out, somewhat pudgy mother who could barely cope with her life's demands. She didn't need Valentine's Day; what she really needed was a day off.

For years, Jack had given her a box of bittersweet chocolate for Valentine's Day. But this year he had forgotten. She couldn't blame him, though. Last week their two youngest had been sick with chicken pox, the toilet had broken, and he had had extra work preparing for this trip. No, these days Jack was also too busy to be anyone's lover. They were Mommy and Daddy now; no wonder he had forgotten to wish her a happy Valentine's Day.

Fifteen hours later, the last child was finally settled in bed, and Meg stumbled to her own room. The house felt suddenly empty, and her heart ached, longing for Jack's presence. She could manage just fine without him, though, she told herself. He hadn't even remembered to call. Her lips tight to hold back the tears, she got ready for bed, wanting sleep and nothing more. "Happy Valentine's Day, Meg," she told herself and flung herself down on the bed.

Her hand fell on something hard beneath the comforter.

Probably a Lego, she thought wearily. . . . But when she flung back the bedcover, she found a small gold-covered box. She sat up, staring at it, then slowly picked it up and opened it. The dark, sweet smell of chocolate filled her nose.

When the phone rang, she knew whose voice she would hear. Smiling, her eyes filled with tears, she picked up the receiver.

"Happy Valentine's Day," Jack said. And his voice told Meg that two exhausted, busy parents could still be lovers.

It is not true that love makes all things easy;
it makes us choose what is difficult.

GEORGE ELIOT

Love is the magician, the enchanter, that changes worthless things
to joy and makes right royal kings and queens of common clay.

ROBERT G. INGERSOLL

Doubt thou the stars are fire;
Doubt that the sun doth move;
Doubt truth to be a liar;
But never doubt I love.

WILLIAM SHAKESPEARE

Dominoes and Kisses

Crash! I dumped the dominoes onto the table and turned over the rectangular pieces. My children and I selected and organized our pieces, hiding the dotted sides from our opponents. We placed the first domino in the center of the table, then took turns matching the dots. Soon we had formed several lines, like trains running across the table.

When my son asked for a kiss as a reward for a particularly good play, I left the table and returned with a dish of chocolate kisses. The children clamored for their portion of "love," and I shared the sweet chocolate with them.

We finished the game and the kisses. After the dominoes were put away, I reminded the kids to brush their teeth.

"That's right," my son drawled. "I need to use my 'love scrubber.' " His nickname for his toothbrush made us laugh until bedtime.

Like matching dominoes end to end, life is a train of connected moments. The deepest pleasure comes from sharing the sweetness with those we love. My son may have used his "love scrubber" to remove the chocolate from his teeth—but for all of us, the sweet memory of that domino game still lingers.

DONNA LANGE

Characteristic of love is its tenderness. . . .
Like a gardener who carefully touches the flowers
to enable the light to shine through and stimulate growth,
the hand of the lover allows for the full expression of the other.

HENRI J. M. NOUWEN

Like the sun,
love radiates and warms into life
all that it touches.

O. S. MARDEN

Love alone is capable of uniting human beings in such a way as to complete and fulfill them, for it alone takes them and joins them by what is deepest in themselves.

PIERRE TEILHARD DE CHARDIN

When my husband was a child, he always knew when the holidays were coming by the bowls of chocolate that appeared around the house. Christmas, Valentine's, Easter–each brought a bounty of brightly wrapped bits of chocolate. All who came to the house were encouraged to take and eat, to savor the rich chocolate. "We are celebrating," those bowls of candy seemed to say. "Our hearts are full of love, and our blessings are bountiful and sweet. Come share with us. Enjoy!"

Intimacy. . .the mystical bond of friendship, commitment, and understanding.

JAMES DOBSON

True love is always costly.

BILLY GRAHAM

Hold tenderly that which you cherish,
for it is precious and a tight grip may crush it.
Do not let fear of dropping it cause you to hold it too tightly:
the chances are, it's holding you, too.

BOB ALBERTI

It is only with the heart that one can see rightly.

ANTOINE DE SAINT-EXUPÉRY

II

Growing the Cocoa Bean

When we share chocolate,
it weaves links between people on many, many levels.

MICHEL RICHART

Chocolate comes from the cacao tree, a tropical plant that thrives in hot, rainy climates. It does not grow well more than twenty degrees north or south of the equator, and it is a delicate and sensitive tree that needs shade and protection from the wind, especially during the first years of its growth. A newly planted cacao seedling is often sheltered by another tree, such as a banana, plantain, coconut, or rubber tree. Once it is well established, though, the cacao tree can grow in full sunlight, so long as it has care and fertile soil.

Like the cacao tree, love only thrives under certain conditions.
It needs to be sheltered, especially when it is young.
Once our love grows deep roots, though,
it too can withstand the sun and wind—
so long as we are careful to nourish it with care and attention.

*It will bloom always fairer,
fresher, more gracious,
because it is a true love,
and because genuine love is ever increasing.
It is a beautiful plant growing
from year to year in the heart,
ever extending its palms and branches,
doubling every season
its glorious clusters and perfumes;
and, my dear life, tell me, repeat to me always,
that nothing will bruise
its bark or its delicate leaves,
that it will grow larger in both our hearts,
loved, free,
watched over, like a life within our life. . . .*

HONORÉ DE BALZAC
to his future wife

The cacao tree is an evergreen, with large glossy leaves that are red when young and green when mature. Moss and bright lichen cling to its bark, and small orchids often grow on its branches. All year long the tree sprouts thousands of tiny pink or white blossoms that cluster along the trunk and older branches. The fruit comes from green or maroon-colored pods that turn to gold and scarlet as they ripen.

The love between two individuals is much the same,
evergreen and life-giving.
Others will be drawn to this love,
for real love is fertile, nourishing. . .
and it makes the world a brighter,
more beautiful place to be.

The job of picking the ripe cacao beans is not easy. The tree is so delicate that the workers cannot risk injuring it by climbing the branches to reach the pods. Instead, the pickers use long-handled, mitten-shaped steel knives to reach the highest pods without wounding the tree's soft bark. Ripe pods are found on trees at all times, since the growing season in the tropics is continuous.

Each pod holds from twenty to fifty cream-colored beans that quickly turn lavender or purple as they are exposed to air. Although each pod holds so many beans, harvesting cacao beans takes time and patience, for approximately four hundred beans are needed to make one pound of chocolate.

Love is also a delicate tree, easily wounded, requiring time and patience before it yields fruit. Its sweet harvest, though, is well worth the effort.

When I think of you, it is like thinking of life. . . .
You are rich and fruitful and glad, and I love you.

D. H. LAWRENCE

We are as we love.
It is love that measures our stature.

WILLIAM SLOANE COFFIN

Many waters cannot quench love,
neither can the floods drown it.

SONG OF SOLOMON 8:7

III

Chocolate's History

Chocolate is not only pleasant of taste,
but it is also a veritable balm for the mouth,
for the maintaining of all glands
and humors in a good state of health.
Thus it is, that all who consume it,
possess a sweet breath.

STEPHANI BLANCARDI (1650–1702)

The divine drink, which builds up resistance and fights fatigue.
A cup of this precious drink permits a man
to walk for a whole day without food.

AZTEC EMPEROR MONTEZUMA (C. 1480–1520)

The first cacao trees grew wild in the rain forests of the Amazon and Orinoco river basins over four thousand years ago. By the seventh century A.D., the Mayans had cultivated these trees; they took them when they migrated to the Yucatan, and there, they paid taxes to the Aztecs with cocoa beans. During Montezuma's regime, a drink made from the beans was considered to be sacred. It could be imbibed only by the male elite, and the beans were used as currency.

When the conquistador Hernando Cortes returned from Mexico in 1520, he introduced his own version of the chocolate drink to the court of King Charles V. When Columbus had tried to impress Europeans with the same drink, they had turned up their noses at the bitter brew, but Cortes caught the King's attention by adding sugar and vanilla to the chocolate. Word of this new drink quickly spread throughout Spain.

Chocolate, when carefully prepared,
is a wholesome and agreeable form of food. . .
is very suitable for persons of great mental exertion,
preachers, lawyers, and above all travelers. . . .
It agrees with the feeblest stomachs,
has proved beneficial in cases of chronic illness. . . .

ANTHELME BRILLAT-SAVARIN (1755–1826)

During the seventeenth and eighteenth centuries, chocolate consumption spread throughout Europe. At first, only the very wealthy could afford it, but the French Revolution also meant that chocolate began to be consumed by common folk as well as the aristocracy. In 1828, the Dutch invented a cocoa press that further reduced the price of chocolate.

Just as the Aztecs had considered chocolate to be sacred, Europeans now thought of chocolate as a therapeutic, health-giving substance. Quaker families in England, such as the Fryes and Cadburies, began producing chocolate, promoting it as "healthful and flesh-forming," a far better alternative to gin.

Chocolate is heavenly, mellow, sensual, deep,
dark, sumptuous, gratifying, potent, dense, creamy. . .
silky, smooth, luxurious, celestial. Chocolate is. . .
happiness, pleasure, love, ecstasy, fantasy. . . .

ELAINE SHERMAN

In 1847, the Fry chocolate factories in Bristol, England molded the first chocolate bar, and in 1850, Richard Cadbury made the first Valentine's Day heart candy box. Milk chocolate was invented in 1879 by two Swiss chocolate manufacturers, Henri Nestle and Daniel Peter. In the United States, Milton Hershey brought mass-production to chocolate manufacturing. He also was the first to experiment with the use of vegetable fats instead of pure cocoa, which raised the melting point of a candy bar. Chocolate could then withstand the heat of American summers—and could also be shipped to troops during World War II.

The U.S. government recognized chocolate's importance to both the nourishment and morale of the Allied Forces—so much so that it allocated valuable shipping space for the importation of cocoa beans. Today, the U.S. Army D-rations still include three 4-ounce chocolate bars.

IV

Chocolate Recipes

*Chocolate melts instantly in the mouth—
an exquisitely pleasurable sensation.
Then the flavors come flooding through—
overwhelming our taste buds with over five hundred of them,
two-and-a-half times more than any other food.
With such a wealth of sensory pleasure in store,
no wonder chocolate should be eaten slowly.*

CHRISTINE MCFADDEN AND CHRISTINE FRANCE

GROWN-UP BROWNIES
(more chocolate, less sugar)

4 ounces unsweetened
  chocolate
½ cup room-temperature
  butter
1½ cups sugar

½ tsp salt
2 tsps vanilla
4 large eggs
⅔ cups flour
1½ cups walnut pieces
  (optional)

Preheat oven to 325 degrees. Grease a 9x9-inch pan. Melt chocolate in a double boiler over simmering (not boiling) water. Let cool to room temperature. Cream the butter and sugar until it is fluffy; add eggs; mix in the melted chocolate; and fold in the flour. Do not over-mix. Bake for 22–25 minutes (17–20 minutes if using a glass pan). Cool before cutting.

Nine out of ten people like chocolate. The tenth person always lies.

JOHN TULLIUS

Easy Chocolate Mousse

6 ounces semi-sweet
chocolate chips
½ cup boiling water

1 egg
1 tsp vanilla
½ pint heavy cream

Blend at high speed in a blender. Pour into dessert dishes and chill for at least an hour.

It has been shown as proof positive that carefully prepared chocolate is as healthful a food as it is pleasant; that it is nourishing and easily digested. . . that it is above all helpful to people who must do a great deal of mental work.

Anthelme Brillat-Savarin (1755–1826)

Chocolate Velvet

½ cup sugar
½ cup unsweetened
cocoa powder
½ cup skim milk
1 envelope unflavored gelatin

⅓ cup water
2 tbsp vanilla
3 egg whites
½ cup sugar

Mix the sugar and cocoa in a pan; add milk and stir while bringing to a boil over medium heat. Sprinkle gelatin over cold water; soften 5 minutes, then add to cocoa mixture with vanilla. Stir well and cool. Beat egg whites on high speed until foamy; add sugar a tablespoon at a time, beating to stiff peaks. Stir eggs into cocoa mixture. Spoon into dessert dishes and chill 2 hours.

If you swallow a generous cup of good chocolate
at the end of the meal,
you will have digested everything perfectly three hours later.

Anthelme Brillat-Savarin

Quick Hot Fudge Sauce

½ cup sugar
½ cup cocoa
½ cup plus 2 tbsp
   evaporated milk (5-ounce can)

⅓ cup light corn syrup
⅓ cup butter or
   margarine
1 tbsp vanilla

Stir together sugar and cocoa in a small saucepan; blend in evaporated milk and corn syrup. Cook over medium heat, stirring constantly until mixture boils. Boil and stir 1 minute; then remove from heat. Stir in butter and vanilla. Serve warm. Makes 1½ cups sauce.

*Two or three hours after a good meal of
three or four dishes of mutton, veal or beef, kid, turkeys
or other foul, our stomachs would be ready to faint,
and so we were fain to support them with a cup of chocolate.*

Thomas Gage, seventeenth century

Uncooked Chocolate Squares

1 pkg chocolate chips
½ cup peanut butter
1 tbsp butter
1 tsp coffee mixed with
  water to make ⅓ cup

1½ cups confectionary
  sugar
1 egg
1 tsp vanilla
3 cups graham crackers,
  broken in small pieces

Melt chips, peanut butter, and butter together. Add coffee and sugar. Mix well and let cool. Add beaten egg, vanilla, and graham crackers. Spread in an 8x8-inch pan. Cover and refrigerate.

The superiority of chocolate, both for health and nourishment, will soon give it the preference over tea and coffee in America.

Thomas Jefferson

BETTER-THAN-ROMANCE

CRUST:
2 cups flour
1 cup nut crumbs

½ cup sugar
½ pound (2 sticks)
    butter

Combine and press into a lasagna pan. Bake at 375 degrees for 15 minutes.

FILLING:
2 packages (6-serving size) instant chocolate pudding
milk according to pudding package directions
⅛ tsp peppermint extract
2 large packages of cream cheese
½ cup confectionary sugar
1 cup heavy cream, whipped

Make the pudding according to directions. Add peppermint extract. Beat the cream cheese with the sugar and half the cream. Layer the cream cheese mixture with the pudding mixture on the crust. Top with the remainder of the whipped cream and sprinkle with nuts.

*M*any of us feel that chocolate is guilty pleasure; our culture worries so much about calories and fat that we're convinced anything that *good* can't be good for us. In fact, though, earlier cultures prized chocolate for its therapeutic value—and they weren't all that far off. A hundred grams of milk chocolate contains 8.4 grams of protein, 220 milligrams of calcium, 55 of magnesium, and 1.6 of iron. It also has zinc, carotene, vitamin E, thiamin, niacin, and folate. And well, yes, it does have 529 calories—but it also offers natural chemicals that help lift our spirits and balance our moods. Its scientific name is *Theobroma cacao*—which literally means "the food of God."

Like chocolate, love is sweet and heady. . .and it nourishes our hearts, for love is of God.

Thank you for the sweetness you bring to my life.